Bobbie Kalman's

...nities

Schoolyard Games

CRABTREE
PUBLISHING COMPANY
WWW.CRABTREEBOOKS.COM

BOBBIE KALMAN & HEATHER LEVIGNE

CRABTREE
PUBLISHING COMPANY
WWW.CRABTREEBOOKS.COM

Created by Bobbie Kalman

For our daughter Caroline Crabtree
and grandchildren Sean, Liam, Charlie, Dexter, and Bonnie
with lots of love. Caroline, a teacher, and the grandkids,
who are students, play lots of school games.
Perhaps they might even invent some of their own.

Editor-in-Chief:
  Bobbie Kalman
Writing team:
  Bobbie Kalman
  Heather Levigne
Managing editor:
  Lynda Hale
Editors:
  Hannelore Sotzek
  Amanda Bishop
  Niki Walker
  Bonnie Dobkin
  Janine Deschenes
Proofreader:
  Crystal Sikkens
Design and photo research:
  Katherine Berti

Photo Credits
Bobbie Kalman: p30
**Genesee Country Village
  and Museum:** p8–9
iStockphoto: helovi, TOC b;
  Cunaplus_M.Faba, p16t;
  JRLPhotographer, p17l;
  p18m; p21b;
Wikimedia Commons: Homer
  Winslow, Snap the Whip, 1872,
  Gift of Christian A. Zabriskie,
  1950, cover; Enic at Ukrainian
  Wikipedia, p16m; Virginia
  State Parks, NT Abby Mae
  with rag doll, p17tr; Manfred
  Heyde, AbnehmfigurFisch,
  p18bl; David J. Fred,Osage

Two Diamonds Jayne Fig 56,
  p18br; Nina Aldin Thune,
  p21t; Nathaniel Currier, After
  Frances Flora Palmer, Brooklyn
  Museum, WinterPastime, 1855,
  p25b; Edward Lamson Henry,
  Yale University Art Gallery, A
  Country School-1948.98, p26;

All other images from Shutterstock

Illustrations and colorizations
Barb Bedell: p4r, p5, p6–7, p9,
  p10, p12–13t, p14, p15, p23,
  p24, p25t, p27, p28–29, p31;
  Bonna Rouse: p4l, 19,

Library and Archives Canada Cataloguing in Publication

Title: Schoolyard games / Bobbie Kalman & Heather Levigne.
Names: Kalman, Bobbie, author. | Levigne, Heather, 1974- author.
Series: Kalman, Bobbie. Historic communities.
Description: [Newly revised edition]. | Series statement: Historic communities |
  Includes index. | Previously published: 2000.
Identifiers: Canadiana (print) 20190233559 | Canadiana (ebook) 20190233567 |
  ISBN 9780778773160 (hardcover) |
  ISBN 9780778773481 (softcover) |
  ISBN 9781427124876 (HTML)
Subjects: LCSH: Outdoor games—North America—History—19th century—
  Juvenile literature.
Classification: LCC GV1200 .K35 2020 | DDC j790.097—dc23

Library of Congress Cataloging-in-Publication Data

Names: Kalman, Bobbie, author. | Levigne, Heather, 1974- author.
Title: Schoolyard games / Bobbie Kalman, Heather Levigne.
Description: New York : Crabtree Publishing Company, [2020] |
  Series: Historic communities | Includes index.
Identifiers: LCCN 2019053230 (print) | LCCN 2019053231 (ebook) |
  ISBN 9780778773160 (hardcover) |
  ISBN 9780778773481 (paperback) |
  ISBN 9781427124876 (ebook)
Subjects: LCSH: Outdoor games--North America--History--19th century--
  Juvenile literature. | Games--History--19th century--Juvenile literature.
Classification: LCC LB3031 .K34 2020 (print) | LCC LB3031 (ebook) |
  DDC 790.1--dc23
LC record available at https://lccn.loc.gov/2019053230
LC ebook record available at https://lccn.loc.gov/2019053231

Crabtree Publishing Company
www.crabtreebooks.com   1-800-387-7650

Printed in the U.S.A./042020/CG20200224

Published in Canada
Crabtree Publishing
616 Welland Ave.
St. Catharines, Ontario
L2M 5V6

Published in the United States
Crabtree Publishing
PMB 59051
350 Fifth Avenue, 59th Floor
New York, New York 10118

Published in the United Kingdom
Crabtree Publishing
Maritime House
Basin Road North, Hove
BN41 1WR

Published in Australia
Crabtree Publishing
Unit 3–5 Currumbin Court
Capalaba
QLD 4157

Contents

Old-time schoolyard games

Hundreds of years ago, education in North America was very different. How children learned often depended on where they lived. Most families in rural communities lived miles apart. Before 1800, children usually learned at home. After that time, one-room schools became more common, especially in northern areas. Children of all ages learned together in a one-room school. Attending school also gave children the opportunity to see their friends daily and play games in the schoolyard. At home, there were just too many chores to do!

Centuries of games

Some of the games the children played had been popular for hundreds of years. Many of them are still popular today, such as tag, Hide-and-Seek, and hopscotch. Over time, some of the rules changed and many games were given new names. One thing that never changed was how much fun they were! Read on to find out what schoolyard games children played in the 1800s!

Who's It?

Just as they do today, many games began with the players choosing someone to be "It." Whoever was It had to chase, tag, or find the other players. Most children did not want to be It. The person who was chosen to be It was decided by using rhyming games.

Count-out rhymes

One way to decide who was It was for everyone to stand in a circle and hold out their fists. One person recited a rhyme and tapped the other players' fists, one after the other, to the beat. When the rhyme ended, the last person to have a hand tapped was out. Eventually, all the players but one were eliminated. The last person holding out a fist became It.

Singing games such as "London Bridge Is Falling Down" and "Ring-Around the Rosie" were popular with younger children.

Children enjoyed playing with hoops. These girls are tossing a hoop using sticks. See page 21 to learn about a game called Graces.

football

shinny

There were different rhymes used to "count out" players.... The person whose hand was tapped on the last word, such as "eevy" or "stink," was out.

One-ery, two-ery,   Ink, pink,
Tick-ery, tee-vy;   Pen and ink;
Hollow-bone,   A study, a stive,
crack-a-bone,   A stove, and
Pen and eevy.   a stink!

This count-out rhyme is a little trickier. The person whose hand is tapped on the word "lie" answers "no" or "yes" and the count continues. The answer made a difference in who was out.

As I went up the apple tree,
All the apples fell on me,
Bake a pudding, bake a pie,
Did you ever tell a lie?
N-O spells "no"
(or Y-E-S spells "yes")
And you are OUT!

In the schoolyard, children played games such as football and shinny, which is like hockey. Other popular games were tag and Hide-and-Seek. This game is called Tug-of-War.

Catch me if you can!

Games of tag have one thing in common—chasing! They are great for getting rid of energy after sitting at a desk for hours. In most games, one person is *It* and must chase the other players. As soon as *It* tags, or touches, someone, the tagged person becomes *It*.

Red Lion

In this game, one person is the "Lion" and another person is the "Lion's Keeper." The Lion selects an area to be a "den" and stands in that spot. The Lion's Keeper stands nearby. The rest of the players walk slowly toward the den and chant, "Red Lion, Red Lion, come out of your den. Whoever you catch will be one of your friends." When the players get close, the Keeper shouts, "Loose!" and the Lion runs out to chase everyone except the Lion's Keeper. If the Lion catches someone, that person must say "Red Lion" three times while holding the tagged player. The tagged player becomes a Lion, and the Lions return to the den. Both players now chase the others. The game continues until all the players have been caught.

Shadow Tag

On sunny days, children enjoyed a game of Shadow Tag. In this game, one person is *It*. Their goal is to step on another player's shadow. If a player's shadow is stepped on, he or she becomes *It*. Players can "hide" their shadows in the shade to take a break, but this is only allowed for a few seconds.

Sticky Apple can be a very funny game! When you are tagged, you must put one hand on the spot where you were touched. Running while holding a hard-to-reach spot, such as your knee or ankle, is not easy to do!

Everybody hide!

Hiding games have always been a childhood favorite. In most hiding games, one player is the seeker while the rest of the players are hiders. Some games, however, are played with only one hider, and everyone else searches for that person. The following games could be played in different ways. But no matter how the games were played, they were always a lot of fun!

Hide-and-Seek

Hide-and-Seek can be played indoors or outdoors, as long as there are enough hiding places. The players decide on a spot to be **home base**. The player who is *It* closes his or her eyes and counts up to a number such as 50 or 100, while the rest of the players hide. When *It* finishes counting, he or she yells, "Ready or not, here I come!" and begins looking for the hidden players.

Home free!

When *It* finds someone, he or she shouts, "One, two, three on (player's name)," and both players run back to home base. If the hider gets to home base first, that person shouts, "One, two, three, home free!" That player is now safe, and *It* must look for the other players. If *It* reaches home first, the player who was caught becomes the new *It* in the next game. Players do not have to wait to be found before they race home— they can sneak home when *It* is not looking. The game continues until all the players have been caught or have made it home safely. If no players get caught, the same person is *It* in the next game.

Think about it

Why would games like tag and Hide-and-Seek have been so popular when groups of children got together?

Kick the Can

Players draw a circle on the ground about six feet (2 m) wide and place an empty can in the center. A shoe can also be used. The person who is *It* must guard the can. The rest of the players stand outside the circle. Suddenly, one person runs into the circle and kicks the can. As *It* retrieves the can, the rest of the players run and hide. When *It* returns to the circle, he or she shouts, "Freeze!" The players must stop immediately and stay where they are.

It calls out the names of the players he or she can see. They must stand near the circle as "prisoners." Then *It* has to find the rest of the players. When *It* leaves the circle, however, a hider can run in and kick the can again to free the prisoners. If there are no prisoners, a hiding player can run into the circle and shout, "Home free!" All the players then run into the circle. The last player inside the circle after "Home free!" is called becomes *It* for the next game.

Whoop!

Many years ago, the game of Hide-and-Seek was also known as Whoop. The seeker did not count to 100. Instead, when the hiders were ready, they called out, "Whoop!"

Sardines

To play Sardines, one person hides while the rest count. When a seeker finds the hider, he or she must hide in the same place without being spotted by the other seekers. Eventually, all but one of the seekers end up crammed into the hiding spot—just like sardines in a tightly packed can! The first seeker to find the hiding spot is the hider in the next game.

In this game of Sardines, the hiding spot is not concealing all the hiders very well! How many children can you see?

Hopping games

Hopping games have always been popular because both young and older children are able to play them. Many of these games began in other countries and were brought over by the settlers. Over time, some of these games changed and new ways to play them were created.

Leapfrog

To play Leapfrog, all the players line up in a row with one player behind the other. The first person in the row bends over in a crouched position, called a back. The next person in line puts his or her hands on the first person's back and leaps over. Then he or she makes a back in front of that player. The next leaper jumps over the first and second backs, one at a time, like a frog. Play continues with each new leaper jumping over the others until he or she reaches the front of the line. The last person in line then leaps over all the other players. The game continues as long as the "frogs" keep hopping!

Keep the Kettle Boiling

This game is a fast version of Leapfrog. As soon as a player jumps over another player's back, he or she crouches down to make a back for the next person. The person over whom the player has leapt, immediately stands up and leaps over the person in front. Many players jump at the same time to keep this game moving quickly.

*When making a back, keep your head tucked under to avoid getting hurt. To make a **low back**, crouch down and hold onto your ankles. For a **little back**, get down on your hands and knees. Leaning forward with your hands on your knees, as shown above, makes a **high back**.*

Hopscotch

Hopscotch is a very old game that dates back to ancient Rome. Romans etched their grids into stone floors, but the settlers drew them on the ground. To play, each player needs a throwing piece called a **potsie** or pitcher. You can use a small stone or even your shoe as the potsie.

Let's get hopping!

To start, a player stands at the beginning of the hopscotch grid and throws the potsie into the first square. The player hops on one foot from one end of the grid to the other, without landing on the square that contains the potsie or stepping on the lines. On single squares, the player hops on one foot. On each double square, however, the player can land with one foot in each square. When the player reaches the end of the grid, he or she turns around on the last square and hops back to the beginning. On the way back, the player must stop in the second block and pick up the potsie from the first one. The player then throws it into the second square and hops from beginning to end again, avoiding the potsie.

Watch your step!

A player continues until he or she makes a mistake, such as throwing the potsie into the wrong block or onto a line, or putting down both feet in a single square. Then the next player takes a turn. At the end of each turn, the potsies stay where they have landed, and the upcoming players must avoid every square that contains one. When it is their turn again, players start where they left off. The game continues until each player has thrown his or her potsie into the last square and has hopped from one end of the grid to the other and back.

Draw your hopscotch grid as shown here. Remember to number each square! You can scratch the grid into the dirt, as settler children did, or draw it on pavement using a piece of chalk.

Skipping games

Skipping was originally a game that boys played, but by the 1800s, it became a game mainly for girls. Children made their own skipping ropes out of grapevines, **hop stems**, or braided straw.

Bringing spring in with a jump

Skipping was a popular activity—especially in spring. In May, settlers planted crops such as corn, potatoes, and wheat. They believed that jumping during planting season would help the crops grow. The higher they jumped, the taller they expected the plants to grow!

Jump, jump, jump a rope,
Merrily in the spring.
Hop, hop on each foot,
As fast as you can sing.

Skipping feet, skipping feet,
Skipping feet all day.
Oh what fun it is to skip,
The whole day away. Hey!

For these two rhymes, turn the rope as fast as possible during the last sentence.

Grizzly bear, grizzly bear,
turn around.
Grizzly bear, grizzly bear,
touch the ground.
Grizzly bear, grizzly bear,
shine your shoes.
Grizzly bear, grizzly bear,
read the news.
Grizzly bear, grizzly bear,
go upstairs.
Grizzly bear, grizzly bear,
say your prayers.
Grizzly bear, grizzly bear,
blow out the light.
Grizzly bear, grizzly bear,
spell good night—
G-O-O-D N-I-G-H-T!

In this skipping rhyme, skippers make the actions described in each line. When spelling "good night," the rope is turned as fast as possible while the skipper tries to spell the entire word without tripping.

Let's play ball!

Ball games were also very popular with children. Most of the balls used were made of wood, cork, or stuffed leather. They were very heavy and did not bounce. The first bouncing balls were made from bull bladders filled with air and covered with leather. These balls were hard, however, and any contact they made with the body was painful. In 1839, toymakers began using rubber to make softer, bouncier balls for children's games, such as Dodge Ball.

Baseball

Baseball is one of most popular sports in North America. It is based on the games of **cricket** and **rounders**, which were played by the British settlers in the 1700s. In rounders, players used a stick to hit a rock and then ran around three posts. Cricket is played with bats, balls, and posts called **wickets**. Players try to score runs by hitting the ball and running between the wickets.

In the 1800s, people began using bats, balls, and bases to play rounders. The game soon became known as baseball.

Aim below the knees, please!

Nine Holes

Each player digs a small hole near a wall, and a line is drawn about 16 feet (5 m) away from the holes. Each player stands near a hole, except one player, who is the pitcher. The pitcher stands on the line and throws a soft ball into one of the holes. When the pitcher gets the ball into a hole, everyone runs away, except the person to whom the hole belongs. This person grabs the ball and throws it at one of the fleeing players. The person who gets hit with the ball becomes the pitcher for the next game. If the thrower misses, however, he or she becomes the pitcher. A player is out of the game after missing three times. The winner is the last person to remain in the game.

Dodge Ball

To play Dodge Ball, players divide into two teams. One team forms a large circle, and the other team stands inside the circle. One person on the team forming the circle starts the game by throwing the ball at a player inside the circle. To prevent anyone from getting hurt, players must aim the ball below the knees and try to hit the other team members on the legs. The players inside the circle move quickly to dodge the ball! When a player is hit, that person joins the other team and becomes part of the circle. The game continues until all the players inside the circle have been tagged with the ball. Players sometimes used two balls to make the game more challenging.

Homemade toys

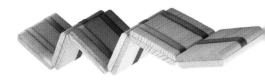

Some children did not own many store-bought toys because their families could not afford them. Materials for toys and games had to be inexpensive and easy to find or make. Some children owned a few basic items such as hoops, balls, marbles, **tops**, and jump ropes. Older children were able to make some of their own toys such as kites and beanbags.

Dolls

Fancy dolls made of wax or porcelain were expensive. Very few girls owned these types of dolls. Instead, most girls had dolls that were handmade from rags or cornhusks. Girls who owned fancy china dolls did not play with them much because these dolls broke easily and were costly and difficult to replace. Rag dolls and corn husk dolls didn't break, and new ones could easily be made.

Wooden toys

Today, most toys are made of **synthetic** materials such as plastic. In the 1800s, handmade toys were made of natural materials such as cotton, dried plant fibers, and wood. Wood was used to make hoops, stilts, building blocks, tops, **whirligigs**, and **Jacob's Ladders**. (Turn to page 30 to make a Jacob's Ladder of your own.) Many older children learned how to **whittle**, or carve, their own toys. The boy on the next page has mastered the skill of walking on homemade wooden stilts.

Settler children played checkers on handmade wooden boards. The checkers were often made of dried, sliced corncobs.

Spinning a whirligig provided hours of fun. You can make your own from a piece of string and a button!

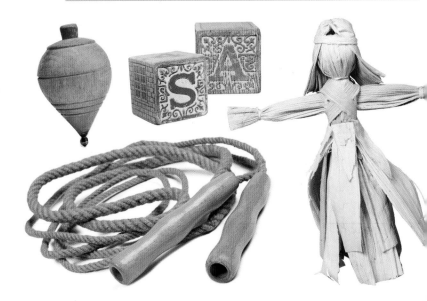

*In many areas, corn was a **staple** food. After the corn was harvested, the husks were dried and used to make dolls for children.*

Homemade kites were made of cloth or paper glued to a wooden frame. A tail was attached to the bottom.

Think about it

Children today are used to store-bought toys and electronics. Why do you think children in the 1700s and 1800s had as much fun with their homemade toys?

17

String games

String games are tricky but fun, and the only equipment needed to play them is a piece of string about five feet (1.5 m) long. Players take turns looping the strings around each other's fingers. In some string games, players use their toes and teeth to pull the strings around their fingers!

An ancient game

String games can be found all over the world and were played in ancient cultures. In North America, Native peoples made string figures of animals such as bears and coyotes, as well as other shapes like the ones you see below. They often used these figures to help them tell stories as they sat around the fire at night.

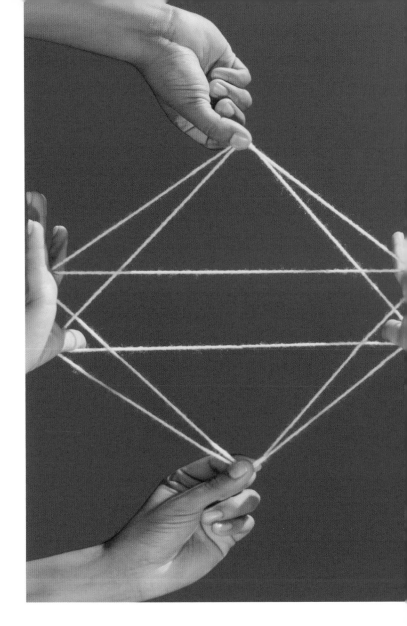

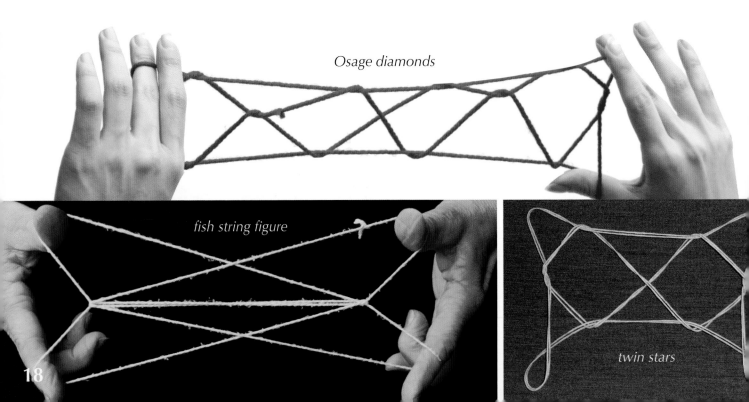

Osage diamonds

fish string figure

twin stars

How to play Cat's Cradle

1 To start **Cat's Cradle**, loop the string around the back of both your hands and pass it through the space between your thumbs and index fingers. Loop the string around each hand again so it crosses your palms. Slide each middle finger under the loop on the palm of the opposite hand. Separate your hands. You will have two crossed strings with one straight string on each side, making the Cat's Cradle design. Hold it out for another person to make the next move. Players take turns making each new design.

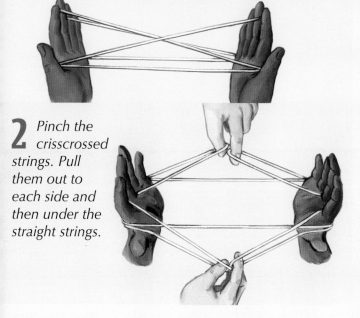

2 Pinch the crisscrossed strings. Pull them out to each side and then under the straight strings.

3 After pulling the strings up through the center, spread your thumbs and index fingers wide apart. This string figure is called the Soldier's Bed.

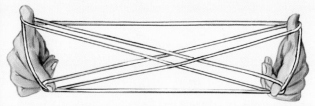

4 Grab the crossed strings and pull them over the side strings and up through the center.

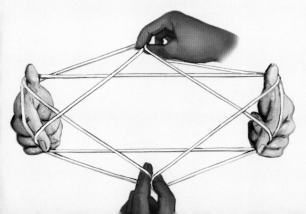

5 Separate your thumbs and index fingers to make Candles. The parallel strings resemble two long, tapered candles.

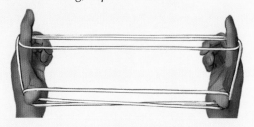

6 Pick up the inside "candle" strings with each little finger. Pull each to the opposite side. With the strings still hooked over your pinkies, draw them over the outside strings and up through the center.

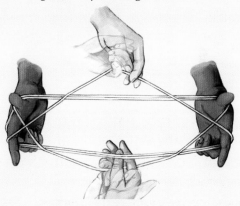

7 This figure is called the Manger. You should still be holding strings on each pinkie finger.

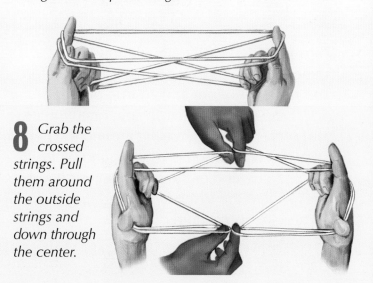

8 Grab the crossed strings. Pull them around the outside strings and down through the center.

9 Your fingers should point downward to make Diamonds, which looks like the Soldier's Bed. What do you think is the next step?

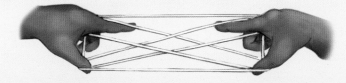

Whirling, twirling tops

Tops provided children with hours of spinning fun! A top is a toy with a wide top and narrow bottom and an iron or wood peg through the center. To spin one kind of top, players wound a string around the peg. They threw their top on the ground while holding one end of the string in their hand. They pulled the string to unwind it, which caused the top to spin.

Peg-in-the-Ring

To play this game, children drew a circle on the ground about three feet (1 m) wide. Players threw their tops into the ring one at a time, trying to peg, or hit, the other tops in the ring. The object of the game was to split an opponent's top.

If a player threw a top and it did not spin or stopped spinning, the top was called "dead." The player could not pick it up to throw it again. Since a dead top was easier to hit than a spinning one, the other players threw their tops at it. If a player pegged a dead top and it bounced outside the ring, it became "live" again. The owner was then allowed to rejoin the game and throw his or her top at the other tops.

Conqueror

Conqueror was an exciting game! Two players spun their tops so that the tops bounced against each other. The top that knocked the other over, but stayed upright itself, was the winner.

Fun with hoops

Wooden hoops were often used in children's games. Hoops were often handmade from wood. A smooth wooden stick about a foot long was also made to help the hoop roll. Some hoops also came from old or broken wagon wheels. These could be wood or metal.

Hoop and stick

Using a stick, children rolled a hoop along the ground as fast as they could. Some children mastered a single hoop and then learned to roll two or more hoops at once! Sometimes they had hoop races to see who could keep their hoop rolling the fastest or farthest.

Through the Hoop

In this competitive game, one person rolled a hoop in a straight line along the ground while one or more players stood about 15 feet (4.5 m) away. The standing players tried to throw their stick through the hoop as it rolled past them. The winner was the player who tossed his or her stick through the hoop the greatest number of times without knocking it down.

© Nina Aldin Thune

Learning how to keep the hoop rolling in a straight line took practice!

playing Graces

Graces

Girls often played Graces, or Grace Hoops, shown left. They developed their balance and coordination by playing this game. Players used sticks to toss a small hoop to each other. They tried to keep the hoop from touching the ground. Catching the hoop on the stick was difficult! To make the game more challenging, girls often played Graces using two hoops, catching both hoops on the same stick at once.

Marble madness!

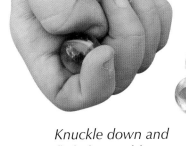

Marble games were popular with people of all ages. In the 1800s, many children owned marbles for playing games in the schoolyard. Some marble games are still played by children today, and marbles now have interesting names, such as "cat's eyes," "swirls," "onionskins," and "clouds."

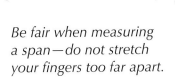

Knuckle down and flick the marble with your thumb.

Be fair when measuring a span—do not stretch your fingers too far apart.

Many kinds of marbles

Some types of early marbles were made of stones that were polished until they were round and smooth. Homemade marbles called **marrididdles** were made of clay. They were left to dry in the Sun until they hardened. Other types of marbles were made of wood, steel, glass, and china.

Marble games

Marble games are divided into three basic types: chase, circle, and hole games. In chase and circle games, players shoot at one another's marbles in a specific area such as a circle drawn on flat ground. In hole games, players shoot their marbles into a hole dug in the ground.

Shooting marbles

If you'd like to try shooting a marble, point your hand down and curl your fingers into your palm. Tuck your thumb behind your index finger. Place a marble in the space between your thumb and finger and **knuckle down**, or rest the knuckle of your index finger on the ground. Flick out your thumb to shoot the marble. Some games require players to use a slightly larger marble as the shooter.

Boss-out

Boss-out, or Hits and Spans, is a simple marble game. Children often played this chasing game on the way to school because it made a long walk much more fun! Only two people are needed to play this game, but more can play. The first player throws a marble ahead a few feet. The second player then shoots his or her marble. If it hits the first player's marble or lands within a **span** of it, the second player wins it. A span is the distance between a player's outstretched thumb and index finger. If the second player does not hit or span the first player's marble, then it is the first player's turn to try and hit the second player's marble.

Marbles today come in many sizes, patterns, and colors. Do you have any marbles that look like these?

Ring Taw

To play Ring Taw, draw a circle about three feet (1 m) wide on the ground and have each player put several marbles inside. Then draw a larger circle about six feet (2 m) wide outside the smaller one. Players choose a starting point on the outer circle from which they will make their first shot.

One person knuckles down and tries to hit a marble inside the ring with a **taw**, or larger, shooting marble. If that person knocks out a marble and the taw also goes out of the ring, he or she keeps the marble that was hit. That player now knuckles down again from the spot where the taw stopped.

If a player misses and the taw rolls out of the inner ring, he or she shoots from that spot on his or her next turn. If the player hits a marble or misses, but his or her taw stays inside the ring, he or she can get back the taw by replacing it with another marble. Players do not like to lose their favorite taw!

Ring Taw is a popular marble game. In this picture, the player is knuckling down before shooting his marble into the ring.

Winter fun

In some areas, winter was a long, cold season. People had more time for leisure activities because they were not able to plant or harvest crops. Playing games kept people entertained during the winter.

Fun in the snow

Children did not let snow stop them from playing games in the schoolyard. In fact, some of their favorite games and activities could be played only in the winter.

Children looked forward to the first snowfall. On sunny days, they played outdoor games of tag such as Fox and Geese. Tobogganing, ice skating, and ice shinny were other fun winter activities.

Many winter schoolyard games kept children warm. Skating, tobogganing, and running were physical activities that helped keep children active and healthy during the winter months.

Tobogganing

After a heavy snowfall, children couldn't wait to use their toboggans! They would pull the long, wooden sleds up to the top of a snow-covered hill, jump on, and then whoosh back down. A rope handle was used to help steer the toboggan and then drag it back uphill.

Fox and Geese

Fox and Geese is a game of tag played in the snow. Using their feet, players mark a large circle in the snow with a smaller circle in the center. Several paths lead out from the inner circle to the outer one, like the spokes of a wheel. The center circle is the "safe" area. One player is the "fox," and the rest of the players are "geese." The fox tries to catch the geese, who must stay on the paths. The geese can run into the center, but if they stay too long, they become trapped! When a goose is tagged, that player becomes the new fox.

Ice shinny

Another popular outdoor game was shinny, which was first played by Native peoples. It later became known as hockey. In summer, they played on a grassy field, and in winter, they played on a frozen river or lake. The teams were made up of 10 to 50 players. Each player had a long, curved stick that he or she used to hit a puck made of rawhide-covered wood or stone. Two logs were placed 130 feet (40 m) apart and were used as goal posts. To score goals, each team tried to shoot the puck between the other team's posts.

Some toboggans were large enough to allow several people to ride downhill at the same time.

Indoor games

In rainy or very cold weather, children could not go outside to play. Luckily, staying indoors could be just as much fun as playing outside. Children played guessing games, word games, and indoor versions of their favorite outdoor games.

Hot Buttered Beans

In this hiding game, an object is "hidden" instead of a person. While the rest of the players cover their eyes, one person places a small object such as a thimble where it is visible but hard to see. When the thimble is placed, the player who hid it calls out, "Hot buttered beans! Please come to supper!" The rest of the players then uncover their eyes and search for the thimble. When players are far from it, the hider says, "Cold." When they get close to the thimble, the hider calls out, "Warm." As the seekers get closer, the hider tells them that they are "warmer." When the searching players are very close, the hider says, "Hot!" The person who finds the thimble hides it the next time.

Gossip

Gossip is played by a group of people. There are many ways to play this game. In one version, one person whispers a sentence into another player's ear, who then whispers it into the next player's ear. The last person who hears the sentence says it out loud. Often, the final version of the original sentence is not only different but also very funny!

I Spy

I Spy is a searching game that is similar to Hot Buttered Beans. To play, one person looks around the room and selects an object but does not tell the rest of the players what it is. The person gives a clue to the players about the object. He or she might say, "I spy with my little eye something that is red." The other children then take turns guessing what the mystery object is by looking for things that are red. Use the clues at the top of the next page to find the objects in the picture. Make up some clues of your own and have a friend guess the names of other objects that you have "spied."

I spy something that is eaten with eggs,
I spy something that has four legs,
I spy something that looks like a mother,
I spy something that is on the little brother.
I spy something that contains a pickle,
I spy something you can buy for a nickel,
I spy something with a round pot belly,
I spy something that is eaten with jelly.

(Turn to page 31 for the answers.)

Think about it

What guessing games do people play today? What makes this kind of game so much fun?

The last day of school

Many schools held games and races on the last day of school. Sometimes, parents, teachers, and students brought some food to have a picnic lunch. Here's your chance to try a few end-of-school activities!

Egg-in-the-Spoon

Each player places an egg on a spoon and lines up in a row. At the starting signal, everyone begins running toward the finish line while balancing his or her egg on the spoon. It is hard to keep an egg on a spoon while running! The winner is the first person to cross the finish line with the egg still on the spoon.

Watch the egg, and it won't drop out!

Think about it

Which games in this book are new to you? Which ones would you like to try?

Three-legged Race

For the Three-legged Race, everyone needs a partner. Tie your right leg to your partner's left leg with a rope. You can also put your right leg into a burlap sack while your partner puts his or her left leg into the sack. When the starter yells, "Go!" you and your partner must run as fast as you can without tripping or falling down. Keeping the same stride as that of your partner is difficult!

Push the Potato

For this race, each player needs a potato to push along the ground. All the players line up in a row. At the starting signal, they begin rolling their potato along the ground with their nose. Players may use only their nose—never their hands—to keep the potato rolling in a straight line. The first person who crosses the finish line wins the race.

Ready, set, go!

What will happen if the girl touches the potato with her hand?

Make a Jacob's Ladder

Not many settler children in early North America had store-bought toys. They had to make their own. One popular toy was the Jacob's Ladder. It was named after a Bible story in which a man named Jacob had a dream. In the dream, he saw a ladder that stretched between Heaven and Earth. Angels were climbing up and down on it.

When you tip the top of a Jacob's Ladder, the block on top seems to tumble down over the blocks beneath it, just like someone climbing down a ladder. The toy is fun to make, and you can use it to perform many tricks and make all kinds of shapes.

What you'll need

- 6 smooth plywood squares, 0.2 inches (0.5 cm) thick and 2.2 inches (5.5 cm) square
- a bit more than 9 feet (2.8 m) of ribbon about 0.2 inches (0.5 cm) wide
- scissors
- wood glue

What you'll do

1. Cut the ribbon into 15 strips, 5.5 inches (14 cm) long. Glue the ribbons, as shown in this picture, to five of the squares.

2. Leave one square plain. When the glue is dry, fold the ribbons underneath, and arrange the squares as shown below.

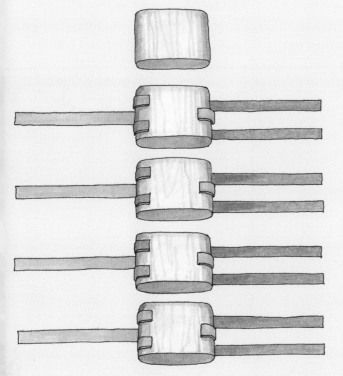

3. Turn one of the squares upside-down.

4. Place a square on top of the upside-down square. Trim the ribbon of the bottom square and glue it to the top one.

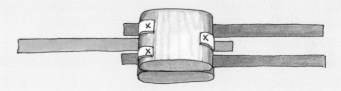

5. When the glue is dry, wrap the ribbon over the top square. Place another square on the top and repeat step 4.

6. Repeat steps 4 and 5 until all the squares have been attached with the ribbon. The plain square is the last one to be attached.

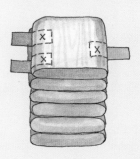

Answers to riddles on page 27:

Ham and sausages are eaten with eggs,
The sleeping cat has four furry legs,
The pretty china figure looks like a Mother,
A bright blue cap is worn by the little brother.

The stout wooden barrel contains a pickle,
Sweet lollipops cost only a nickel,
The black iron stove has a round pot belly,
Cupcakes and cookies are eaten with jelly.

Glossary

Note: Some boldfaced words are defined where they appear in the book.

Cat's Cradle A game played with a long piece of string in which two or more players use a series of hand movements to create string designs

high back A position in Leapfrog in which a player bends forward slightly from the waist and holds his or her knees

home base A place from which a game begins; a game's goal or endpoint

hop stems The long stems of the hop plant, which the settlers used for making jump ropes

Jacob's Ladder A toy made of several flat blocks of wood connected with ribbon, which appear to tumble down when held in the air

knuckle down Describing the position of the hand when preparing to shoot a marble

little back A position in Leapfrog in which a player bends forward and holds onto his or her ankles

low back A position in Leapfrog in which a player gets down on his or her hands and knees

marrididdle Handmade clay marbles

potsie An object, such as a small stone or pine cone, that is used as a marker in hopscotch. During the 1800s in New York, children called the game of hopscotch "potsie."

rounders A game that was similar to baseball, in which players hit a rock with a stick and ran around posts

shinny In this game, originally played by Native peoples, players use long sticks to hit a ball between two goal posts. Shinny is played on ice or on a field.

span The distance measured between the thumb and index finger

staple A main product of a place

synthetic Describing something that is made from materials not found in nature

taw A marble, often a larger one, that a player uses to shoot at other marbles in a game

top A small wooden toy, narrow at one end and wide at the other, which spins when it is thrown on the ground

whirligig A spinning toy made from a length of string threaded through a hole in a round piece of wood

Index